P9-DBT-416

Baby on the Way

William Sears, M.D., Martha Sears, R.N.,
and Christie Watts Kelly

Illustrated by Renée Andriani

LB
1837

wn and Company ❧ Boston New York London

To the eight times we've had a baby on the way —
to Jim, Bob, Pete, Hayden, Erin, Matt, Stephen, and Lauren
— *W. S.* and M. S.

For my wonderful husband, Shawn, who makes it all possible
— C. W. K.

For my sisters Cyndy DaSilva and Marnie Augustine, who keep me smiling
— R. A.

Text copyright © 2001 by William Sears, Martha Sears, and Christie Watts Kelly
Illustrations copyright © 2001 by Renée Andriani

First Edition

Library of Congress Cataloging-in-Publication Data

Sears, William, M.D.
Baby on the way / by William Sears and Martha Sears, with Christie Watts Kelly ; illustrated by Renée Andriani.—1st ed.
p. cm.
Includes bibliographical references.
ISBN 0-316-78767-1
1. Pregnancy—Juvenile literature. 2. Childbirth—Juvenile literature. 3. Infants
(Newborn)—Juvenile literature. [1. Pregnancy. 2. Babies.] I. Sears, Martha. II. Kelly,
Christie Watts. III. Williams-Andriani, Renée, ill. IV. Title.
RG525.5 .S42 2001
618.2'4—dc21
00-038451

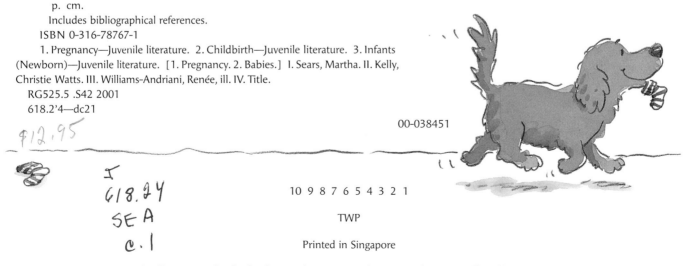

10 9 8 7 6 5 4 3 2 1

TWP

Printed in Singapore

The illustrations for this book were done in Lumadye on Strathmore 140lb. cold press paper.
The text was set in Joanna and Angie, and the display type is Forte MT.

NOTES FOR PARENTS AND CAREGIVERS

Parents and caregivers will find it helpful to preview this book and read these notes before sharing the book with a child. The text and illustrations reflect a responsive parenting style known as Attachment Parenting. (See "About Attachment Parenting" on page 32.)

❧ Since pregnancy and birth choices are very individual, we encourage you to modify the text as you read to your child, according to the choices you will be making surrounding these important events.

❧ The amount of detail children need to know will vary with their age and maturity level. While it's important to be accurate, children don't need — or necessarily want — to know every detail.

❧ Use the words that are most familiar to your child, or the words you feel most comfortable using. The "Answers for the Very Curious" sidebars should give you some ideas of child-friendly ways to explain complex events to your child.

❧ Children are often fascinated by the things babies can do while they're still in the womb — sleep, suck their fingers or thumbs, move their arms and legs, touch their toes, play with their umbilical cord, hear the sound of voices, do somersaults, and even move to the rhythm of music! Talking to children about these things throughout the pregnancy can make the baby seem more real to them.

❧ To focus on the older child's new status as an older brother or sister, consider having the child help you make and send out "older brother" or "older sister" announcements along with (or instead of) baby announcements.

❧ Help make the birth seem more appealing by preparing a "gift from the baby" ahead of time. Also have some small gifts to use when visitors forget to bring a gift for the older child, and allow the older child to open gifts brought for the baby.

❧ Depending upon the age and temperament of your older child, you may plan to have him or her there for the actual birth. Shared experience draws people closer, and a special bonding takes place among people who participate in a baby's birth. After seeing how much hard work and joy surrounds the big event, siblings can have a greater acceptance and appreciation of the baby. If you do plan to have an older child at the birth, assign a friend or relative to take care of him or her. (If more than one child is present, an adult should be assigned for each child.) Prepare the child for the realities of birth, such as the mother making noises or being red-faced and sweaty when she pushes. Explain that there will be "okay blood," not "hurt blood." Obtain appropriate videos of normal vaginal deliveries from a childbirth instructor or an organization such as ICEA (see "Resources" on page 32) and watch them with your child, after previewing them yourself.

When a new baby grows inside your mommy, her belly isn't the only thing that is changing and growing.

How does it feel for your mommy? It feels like love is growing inside her, and it makes her very hungry. Hungry like you feel at lunchtime, right before you take the first bite of your peanut butter sandwich.

It makes her thirsty, too. Thirsty like you feel when you eat *sooo* many pretzels and your mouth is *sooo* dry that you have to hurry to get a drink of water.

Sometimes it makes her feel tired. Tired like you feel when you've been running and jumping and playing at the park all day, and you can barely keep your eyes open.

It might make her feel like building a cozy nest for your family. Like when you spend a rainy morning building a fort out of blankets and boxes, just so you can snuggle down all safe from the storm.

It can make your mommy's tummy feel yucky, too. Like the

way your tummy feels yucky when you eat three slices of

birthday cake and ice cream. That's when your mommy needs

you and your daddy to bring her a cracker and some fizzy

water — maybe you can have some, too.

And, sometimes, it makes her feet hurt. Owie! Just like your feet feel when you squeeze them into last year's shoes. That's when you and your daddy can remind her to put her feet up and rest, and you can set the table for dinner.

As the baby gets bigger and bigger, your mommy's lap gets smaller and smaller. But there's always room for you on your mommy's lap. Just ask her; she'll show you.

Exciting things are happening in your mommy's belly, inside a baby holder called a uterus. The tiny baby gets bigger and busier each day!

WHAT YOU CAN DO

🐟 Visit the doctor or the midwife with your mommy and listen to the baby's heartbeat.

🐟 Look at pictures of babies growing inside their mommies' bellies.

🐟 Ask your mommy what it felt like when *you* were growing inside her.

Your home is changing — making room for baby.

Love is growing in your home.

You are growing up — becoming

an older brother or sister.

Just put your hand on your mommy's belly bulge. Can you feel the baby moving inside, all bumpy and lumpy? It's crowded in there, kind of like being in a sleeping bag with the zipper all zipped up.

Just put your mouth right up to your mommy's belly and talk to your baby brother or sister. The tiny baby loves to hear you and your mommy and your daddy talking and singing all day long.

Just hug your mommy's belly.

The tiny baby can feel your love

— and so can your mommy.

WHAT YOU CAN DO

🐝 Look at pictures of when you were a tiny baby.

🐝 Draw a picture of what your baby might look like.

🐝 Help your mommy and daddy think of a name for the baby.

🐝 See if you have any toys or clothes that you can share with the baby.

You can help your mommy and daddy make room for the baby in your home. You will need a special place for the baby to sleep, a place for the baby's clothes, and a place to change the baby's diaper.

When the baby has finished growing inside your mommy, then the baby is ready to come out. Your mommy's uterus tells her it's time by starting to squeeze. Her belly will feel as hard and tight and round as a big ball, and she will need to take some deep breaths. When that happens, you can help her by being as quiet as a mouse.

After your mommy has lots and lots of belly squeezes, called contractions, it will be time for her and your daddy to go to the place where the baby will be born. Other people — doctors, midwives, and nurses — will be there to help, because it will be hard work for your mommy.

WHAT YOU CAN DO

🐝 When your mommy's uterus starts working to squeeze the baby out, her belly is "making a muscle." Can you make a muscle with your arm?

🐝 Babies need to wear diapers instead of going to the potty. Can you change a diaper on a baby doll?

🐝 Babies are too little to hold up their own heads. Can you hold a doll the way babies need to be held — with your hand behind the doll's head?

BIRTHING CENTER

ANSWERS FOR THE VERY CURIOUS

How does the baby get out? There is an opening called a vagina between your mommy's legs. It is a soft tunnel for the baby to move through to get out. The door to this opening, called the cervix, is usually closed tightly. But when the baby is ready to be born, the door opens up and helps your mommy push the baby through. It's a small door, so it takes a lot of work for the baby to squeeze through, kind of like having a very tight turtleneck sweater pulled over your head.

Why is your mommy's belly squeezing? At first the squeezes, called contractions, are opening the door to the uterus so the baby can come out. Then the contractions start to push the baby through the door. It takes a long time to open the door and a long time for the baby to squeeze through!

Your mommy and daddy will be very busy while the baby
is being born, so they will plan something special for you
to do. You might visit with a friend, an aunt, an uncle, a
grandma, or a grandpa (and maybe even spend the night).

But no matter how busy your mommy is,

she will be thinking of you — wherever she goes

and wherever you are. Because you are always

special in your mommy's heart.

While you're waiting for the baby to come, you can plan the baby's Birth Day party, make the baby a Birth Day card, and wrap a special gift for the baby. Before you know it, you will meet your new baby brother or sister.

The baby will cry. Sometimes a lot, sometimes a little.

Sometimes loudly, sometimes softly.

That's how babies tell us what they need.

Your mommy will hold the baby a lot of the time. Tiny babies just sleep and nurse all day long — nursing is how babies get milk from their mommies' breasts.

You can hold the baby, too. Your mommy and daddy will help

you hold the baby very carefully. You can talk softly to your baby.

The baby will even remember the sound of your voice!

ANSWERS FOR THE VERY CURIOUS

☙ Why is the baby so wrinkly? The baby has been floating in something like water in your mommy's uterus for nine months. Think about how wrinkly your fingers and toes get when you take a long, warm bath.

☙ Why are the baby's eyes squinty? The baby has been in the dark for nine months. Everything looks bright to the baby, just like when you first wake up in the morning and turn on the light.

☙ What's that thing on the baby's belly? That's left over from the umbilical cord, a special tube that fed the baby inside your mommy. It will soon fall off, and you'll be able to see the baby's belly button!

☙ Why is the baby all curled up in a little ball? The baby has been curled up like that inside the uterus for a long time. That's how the baby feels best.

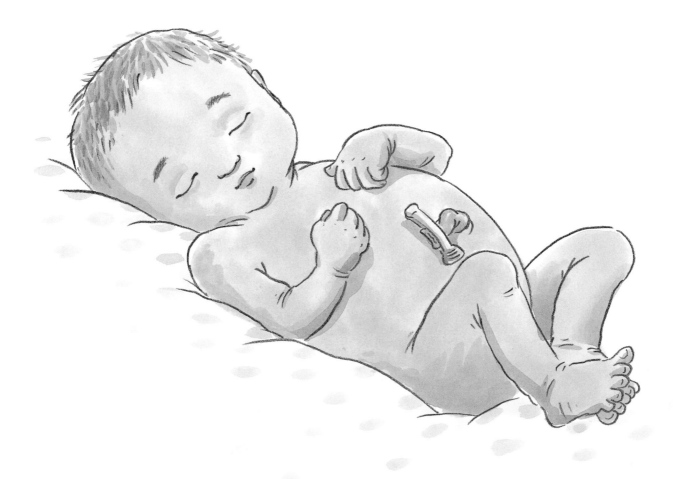

By now you may be wondering when you're finally going to meet your new baby. You might be tired of talking about it and reading about it. You might feel like you've been waiting *forever*. But once upon a time, YOU were the baby growing inside your mommy's belly. And everyone felt the same way waiting for you.

Soon your new baby will be here for you to love, too.

About Attachment Parenting

Attachment parenting is a *responsive* style of parenting that helps facilitate a child's secure emotional attachments. When parents understand, anticipate, and meet their children's needs in a developmentally appropriate way, they establish a warm, connected relationship based on love and trust.

Connectedness, love, and *trust* — but not permissiveness — are keys to the attachment parenting concept of discipline. When parents model desirable behavior and set boundaries and consequences based on readiness, children tend to behave appropriately out of a desire to please rather than from fear of punishment.

Attachment parenting is an *approach,* rather than a strict set of rules. It's the way many people parent instinctively — comforting a crying baby, showing an older child a constructive way to vent frustrations, guiding children to independence by providing a secure base. The following "Five Baby Bs" are attachment parenting tools that can help parents and babies get connected right from the start.

1. Birth bonding: Babies need to continue feeling connected after birth, no matter what kind of birth situation. Planning ahead to allow skin-to-skin contact with mom and dad, breastfeeding, and rooming-in with your baby if at the hospital will set the stage for a good start to the parenting relationship.

2. Breastfeeding: Human milk is the best food for baby humans. Breastfeeding as soon as possible after birth gives the optimal chance for a good start. Continuing as long as possible helps both baby and parents reap the most benefits.

3. Babywearing: Carried babies are more content and less fussy, giving them more quiet and alert time for cognitive and physical development. Being physically close to baby helps parents learn to read baby's signals and develop intuition about baby's needs.

4. Being flexible in sleeping arrangements: Babies need to be close to parents at night as well as the daytime. Co-sleeping (sleeping in the same bed or the same room) can be an effective way to satisfy a baby's needs as well as to make life easier for a nursing mother. It also helps working parents reconnect with their children after being separated all day.

5. Belief in the language value of a baby's cry (and other cues): Since infants can't talk, their only means of communication are through body language and crying. Parents learn to read their baby's body language and pre-cry signals as well as their cries and respond appropriately to the baby's needs, helping baby develop trust and communication skills.

Resources

www.askdrsears.com is an interactive Web site where you can ask — and find the answers to — your toughest parenting questions.

www.parenting.com features articles by William and Martha Sears.

The Sears Parenting Library, by William Sears, M.D., and Martha Sears, R.N.
The Pregnancy Book: Everything You Need to Know from America's Baby Experts, written with Linda Hughey Holt, M.D., F.A.C.O.G.
The Birth Book: Everything You Need to Know to Have a Safe and Satisfying Birth
The Breastfeeding Book: Everything You Need to Know About Nursing Your Child From Birth Through Weaning
The Baby Book: Everything You Need to Know About Your Baby — From Birth to Age Two
The Fussy Baby Book: Everything You Need to Know — From Birth to Age Five
The Discipline Book: Everything You Need to Know to Have a Better-Behaved Child — From Birth to Age Ten
The Family Nutrition Book: Everything You Need to Know About Feeding Your Children — From Birth Through Adolescence
The A.D.D. Book: New Understandings, New Approaches to Parenting Your Child, written with Lynda Thompson, Ph.D.

Attachment Parenting International (API) is a member organization networking with attachment parents, professionals, and like-minded organizations around the world. In addition to parent support groups, the organization provides educational and research materials. 1508 Clairmont Place, Nashville, TN 37215, USA; www.attachmentparenting.org; 615-298-4334.

La Leche League International (LLLI) is the world's foremost authority on breastfeeding, offering breastfeeding support groups in cities worldwide, one-on-one help for breastfeeding mothers, and a catalog of products and literature. 1400 North Meacham Road, Schaumburg, IL 60173-4048, USA; www.lalecheleague. org; 847-519-7730; 800-LA-LECHE (525-3243).

American Academy of Husband-Coached Childbirth® **(The Bradley Method® of Natural Childbirth);** Box 5224, Sherman Oaks, CA 91413-5224, USA; www.bradleybirth.com; 800-4-A-BIRTH (422-4784).

International Childbirth Education Association, Inc. (ICEA); P.O. Box 20048, Minneapolis, MN 55420, USA; www.icea.org; 952-854-8660.

Lamaze International; 1200 19th Street Northwest, Suite 300, Washington, DC 20036-2422; www.lamaze.org; 800-368-4404.